AROUND THE WORLD IN 80 WAYS

ILLUSTRATED BY KATY HALFORD

1 DUGOUT BOAT

The earliest boats in history were built from wooden tree trunks, which were hollowed out with flint tools or fire. People also made simple rafts using logs tied together with rope. Early boats were used for fishing and trading goods.

2 HORSE

Thousands of years ago horses were tamed so they could be ridden and used for pulling chariots and carts. Horses are tough and move fast, so people could now travel much quicker over longer distances, send messages, and carry goods.

3 ANCIENT CHARIOT

Early chariots must have been a fearsome sight in battle. Pulled by teams of speeding horses, warriors stood on a raised platform and hurled spears, fired arrows, or slashed with swords. Chariots were also raced for sport.

4 ▷ LITTER

A litter was a chair, often covered, fixed to poles that were carried between two men. Traveling in litters used to be very popular, especially with rich people who didn't want to walk in dirty, muddy streets.

5 ▷ STAGECOACH

Stagecoaches were so-called because their horses were changed every few miles to keep them fresh, so the journey was made in "stages." These were the most common form of public transportation until the arrival of the steam train.

6 FIRST STEAM TRAIN

A steam train burns coal to heat water and create the steam that powers the engine, with the fireman constantly having to shovel coal onto the fire. The world's first public railroad was opened in 1825 with a steam engine called Locomotion No.1, which could travel at 15mph (24kph).

7 ▷ GO-KART

Go-karts are small, four-wheeled vehicles that are powered either by the driver pedaling or by a gas-powered engine. Some people build their own go-karts using tires, tubing, and even parts from lawnmowers!

8 ▷ DONKEY

Donkeys are probably the oldest type of pack animal—they have been used to carry heavy loads for thousands of years. Donkey rides are a traditional attraction for children at beach resorts in the United Kingdom.

9 ▷ SURFBOARD

The sport of surfing is very popular all over the world, especially in countries where there are huge waves. Surfers stand up on their boards and try to "catch" a wave to ride along while trying to keep their balance.

10 FUNICULAR RAILWAY

The two cars on a funicular railway counterbalance each other—the one going down helps pull the other one up. They are pulled by a cable that runs around a pulley wheel at the top of the track.

11 KITEBOARD

Kiteboarding is an all-action watersport. Using a huge power kite and a specially shaped board, the surfer harnesses the power of the wind to ride the waves and travel at high speeds across the water.

12 BICYCLE

It is estimated that there are more than a billion bicycles in the world! Environmentally friendly and a great way of staying healthy, bikes are used to travel short distances to school or work, and for exercise and sport.

13 MOTORCYCLE

There are many different motorcycles, including sport bikes for fast riding, touring bikes for long journeys, and dirt bikes for off-road adventures. Shiny choppers with extra-long forks just look so cool!

14 ▷ UNICYCLE

You need great balance to ride a unicycle because it has just one wheel and no handlebars for steering. Unicycles are often seen at circuses and carnivals, and they are also ridden by street performers.

15 ▷ TANDEM

A tandem is a bicycle built for two, with the seats positioned one behind the other on the frame. The rider in front steers, but both people do the pedaling. Some tandems have more than two seats—there's even one for eight people!

16 ▸ DINGHY

Dinghies are small, open sailboats for one or two people. They are simple to operate, so perfect for learning to sail. Since dinghies are light, they can zip across the water super-fast and are lots of fun.

17 ▸ BOWTOP WAGON

Also known as a "vardo," a bowtop wagon is a traditional horse-drawn vehicle. Outside, the wagons are beautifully decorated, while inside they feature a bed, a wardrobe, and a stove with a chimney to let the smoke out.

18 TRACTOR

Tractors are designed to pull heavy machinery. They are usually used by farmers to carry out jobs that require lots of effort, such as plowing fields, planting seeds, and harvesting crops.

19 CANAL BOAT

For hundreds of years, canals—which are human-made waterways—have been used to transport goods. Canal boats were originally built as working boats, but are now mostly used for vacations on the water, or even as family homes.

20 ⟩ TRAIN

Every day millions of people worldwide use trains to travel to work, visit family, or go on vacation. Trains are more environmentally friendly, safer, and faster than cars—there are no traffic jams when you travel by train!

21 ⟩ BUS

Modern-day versions of horse-drawn carriages, buses are designed to take passengers on both short and long-distance journeys. Some are basic, while others are very comfortable, with reclining seats, folding tables, televisions, and bathrooms.

㉒ TRAM

Trams are a type of public transportation featuring cars that run on rails through city streets. The earliest trams were pulled by horses, but today most are powered by electricity carried in overhead cables.

23 ▷ TAXI

The great thing about taxis is that, rather than having to start and finish at a station or bus stop, they can take you wherever you want, whenever you want. Some taxis are ordered ahead, while others pick up customers on the street.

24 ▷ SELF-BALANCING SCOOTER

A self-balancing scooter can transport a person along at a speed of 12.5mph (20kph), which is about four times as fast as walking. Some police in the United States use them while on patrol.

25 DOUBLE-DECKER BUS

Inside a double-decker bus a staircase links two levels of seats. Sometimes the top deck is open and the bus is used for sightseeing tours. Double-decker buses are used all over the world, but the most famous is the red London bus.

26 SUBWAY

Subways carry people across towns and cities, often through tunnels or on tracks high above the streets. The stations are short distances apart, making it easy for passengers to travel to many different places.

27 CAR

The earliest cars were known as "horseless carriages" and were powered by steam, electricity, or gasoline. Only rich people were able to buy cars until the early 1900s, when Henry Ford's Model T became the first affordable car.

When it was discovered that the gases released by motor engines were bad for our health and the environment, carmakers began to develop models powered by electricity and other cleaner fuels. It is hoped that this will be the future for all cars.

Cars changed the way people lived their lives. They could now travel anywhere they wanted—to work, to visit friends, or to go on vacation. As time went by, cars became a safer and more reliable form of personal transportation.

There are now millions of cars on the planet. Many are used for work and transportation, while others are designed for pleasure and fun. For example, sports cars combine speed and style for an exhilarating ride.

28 LIFEBOAT

Lifeboats are designed to help rescue people in trouble at sea. Quick, powerful, and easy to steer, they can stay afloat in rough waters. With lots of safety equipment onboard, they are prepared for any emergency.

29 WATER SCOOTER

With its handlebars and seat for two, a water scooter looks like a motorcycle on the water. Yet rather than its engine powering wheels, it helps it to squirt a jet of water out the back so this fun craft can zip across the surface at high speed.

30 SUBMARINE

Submarines are vessels that can travel underwater as well as on the surface. Some submarines can dive down to the ocean floor, where scientists can study rarely seen fish and other deep-sea creatures.

31 FERRY

Ferries transport people and vehicles across rivers and lakes, and over short distances at sea. These boats are large enough to carry hundreds of cars, trucks, and passengers, while some can even transport trains!

32 HOVERCRAFT

A hovercraft uses special blowers to inflate a huge cushion of air under the craft so that it can travel over bumpy ground and across water. Hovercrafts are used as ferries, for sightseeing trips, and by the emergency services.

19

33 HOT-AIR BALLOON

Hot-air balloons work by heating the air inside a balloon with a burner. As hot air rises, the balloon is lifted off the ground. To land, air is let out of the balloon so that it sinks to the ground.

In 1783 the Montgolfier brothers launched a hot-air balloon carrying two people. It was the first time humans had successfully taken to the air. On the test flight the basket had contained a sheep, a duck, and a rooster!

The first hot-air balloon flight across the Pacific Ocean was made by the Virgin Otsuka Pacific Flyer in 1991 when it flew from Japan to Canada. The journey took 46 hours 15 minutes in what was the biggest balloon ever built.

Balloons are used on safari trips in Africa to get amazing views of the landscape and the wildlife. They are so quiet that they float gently above the animals without disturbing them.

34 SPEEDBOAT

Large engines in a speedboat enable it to travel super-fast across the water. These powerful boats are used for racing, deep-sea fishing, and for sports like water-skiing, while they are also used by the emergency services.

35 GONDOLA

A gondola is a flat-bottomed rowboat found in Venice, Italy. Since the city is built on many small islands, there are very few roads or cars, so this is one of the best ways to get around. The gondolier stands at one end of the boat and moves it with a long oar.

36 VAPORETTO

Vaporettos are waterbuses that travel on set routes along the waterways and canals of Venice. Many of the thousands of tourists who visit Venice each year use vaporettos to see the city's beautiful sights.

37 KAYAK

Kayaks are small, narrow boats for one or two people, who use paddles to propel the craft across the water. The word "kayak" means "hunter's boat," and they were originally were used for fishing and hunting.

38 ▶ SNOWMOBILE

A snowmobile looks a little bit like a motorcycle, but with short skis instead of a front wheel and powered tracks at the back to move through the snow and ice. Snowmobiles are an important form of transportation for people living in cold, snowy countries.

39 ▶ DOG SLED

Dogsleds have been used for hundreds of years for taking people and supplies across the ice and snow. Husky dogs are the perfect breed for this because they are strong and fast, with thick fur and padded paws to help them survive in freezing conditions.

40 ▶ SNOWCAT

These powerful vehicles are designed to travel through the deepest snow and up the steepest slopes! Rough or slippery ground is no problem for a snowcat's wide, rubber tracks, and they are ideal for mountain rescue missions.

41 ▶ SLEIGH

A sleigh is a large, open-topped carriage that is pulled by horses or sometimes by reindeer! Instead of wheels, a sleigh has large runners as you would find on a sled, which glide over slippery snow and ice.

25

42 SKI LIFT

It's easy to slide down a mountain, but getting back up is hard work! This is where a ski lift can help. Hop on one of the chairs fixed to a cable constantly moving between a set of towers and you will soon return to the mountaintop.

43 SNOWBOARD

A snowboard is like a short, wide ski. With both feet attached to the board, a snowboarder leans forward, backward, and side to side to move, stop, and turn. Some snowboarders can do sensational tricks and incredible jumps.

44 SKIS

Skis are long, narrow blades that fasten onto special boots. They are perfect for speeding down snowy slopes and across icy ground. Downhill and cross-country skiing are popular winter sports in mountainous regions.

45 ICE SKATES

Around 5,000 years ago, humans figured out that it was quicker to slide across the ice, so they made basic skates made from animal bone. Today, skates are made from steel allowing you to whiz across the ice.

46 MICROLIGHT

Microlights are very light aircraft
with one or two seats that can fly at
speeds of up to 100mph (161kph). They may not
look very tough, but they are strong aircraft—some
have even been flown all the way around the world.

47 CABLE CAR

Cable cars are used to transport people
up and down mountains using cabins
suspended on huge cables. A powerful
motor at the bottom of the mountain
pulls one cabin up and at the same time
the other cabin goes down.

48 WHITEWATER RAFT

Whitewater rafting is an exciting activity
where people paddle down fast-flowing
rivers in an inflatable raft. It is called
"whitewater" because the river is all
churned up where it flows fastest over
rocks in what are known as "rapids."

49 HANG GLIDER

Suspended in a harness underneath a huge wing similar to a kite, a hang glider pilot uses thermals (columns of rising air) to fly through the air. To take off, the pilot runs along to launch his glider from a high place such as the top of a hill.

50 ZIP LINE

One end of a zip line is higher than the other, so a person can slide down it on a harness or pulley. Small zip lines can be found in playgrounds, but people can also ride them in rain forest canopies or across deep gorges.

51 > CAMEL

For thousands of years people have used camels to travel across hot, dry regions—they have earned the nickname of "ships of the desert." Camels can be ridden or used to carry luggage, and can reach speeds of up to 40mph (65kph.)

Camels are perfect for traveling across deserts. They store fat in their humps for energy when there's little food or water, their bushy eyelashes and special eyelids protect their eyes from the sand, and their nostrils can close shut.

There are two types of camel. A camel with one hump is a dromedary or Arabian camel, found in North Africa and the Middle East, while a camel with two humps is a Bactrian camel from Central Asia.

A long line of camels traveling together along a regular route and carrying passengers or goods is known as a "camel train" or a "caravan." In ancient times camel trains were an important way for people to trade with each other.

52 ▸ ELEPHANT

Elephants are strong and sure-footed, so they are great for traveling over bumpy ground. These beautiful creatures used to be used in ceremonies and for hunting, but today they are mainly working animals.

53 ▸ CYCLE RICKSHAW

Cycle rickshaws are a common sight in Asia, but they are also used all over the world in cities where people need to travel short distances quickly. The bicycle is attached to a wheeled cart that carries one or two passengers.

54 ▷ TUK-TUK

A tuk-tuk is a motorized version of a rickshaw that's used as a form of transportation in countries such as Thailand, India, and China. Also known as an auto rickshaw, it got its name from the "tuk tuk" sound of the engine.

55 ▷ SCOOTER

Scooters are cheap to buy, easy to ride, and great for zipping through busy traffic in crowded cities. Although they look similar to motorcycles, their smaller engines mean that they can't go as fast. However, they are much easier to maneuver!

56 ▷ MAGLEV

On a maglev (or magnetic levitation) train, huge magnets underneath the carriages interact with a magnetic force on the track so the train "floats" over the rails and travel super-quick. A Japanese maglev reached 375mph (603kph), making it the fastest train in the world.

57 ▷ QUAD BIKE

Quad bikes are perfect vehicles for riding over rough ground. Farmers use them to check on their animals in faraway fields, while others race them in the desert, on ice, and over muddy tracks.

58 > STREETCAR

The original streetcars were developed to transport people up the steep city hills of San Francisco, USA. An operator uses a strong grip to attach the streetcar to a constantly moving cable under the street so the car can be pulled along.

59 > IN-LINE SKATES

These are called in-line skates because the wheels attached to the boots are arranged in line. They were first used for playing ice hockey in warm summer months, then people began to use them for fun and exercise.

60 STEAMBOAT

Steamboats use steam to power propellers or large paddles fitted onto the sides or the back of the boat. Until around a hundred years ago, they were a common sight on rivers and lakes, transporting passengers and goods along the water.

61 ROWBOAT

In a rowboat, the rower sits in the middle of the boat facing backward and pulls the oars through the water. In the days of sailing ships, oars were important because if there was no wind then sailors could row the boat instead.

62 YACHT

Yachts are used for sports and recreation, from small yachts used for short day trips, to huge luxury yachts with cabins, kitchens, and everything needed for a long journey. Some large yachts race against each other around the world.

63 PEDALO

Pedalos use pedal-powered paddles to move across the water. They are mainly found in lakes or on calm seas, although in 2018 a team of friends became the first people to cross the Atlantic by pedalo—a distance of 3,000 miles (4,828km)!

64 POGO STICK

A pogo stick is a pole with a spring inside it—a rider stands on the footrests and jumps up and down. Pogo sticks are mostly used for fun in a backyard or park, but some people also do cool stunts and tricks with them.

66 SPACE HOPPER

First introduced in the 1970s, space hoppers are large, air-filled rubber balls that you sit on and bounce, with handles on top to help keep your balance. They are also known as moon hoppers or hoppity hops.

65 SKATEBOARD

The idea of skateboarding may have come about when some surfers decided to find a way to surf on land as well as in the ocean! Skateboarding is now popular around the world—many towns have special skate parks with ramps and jumps.

67 RIDE-ON SCOOTER

Many years ago children used to make their own scooters using wood or scrap materials. Scooters are still popular today, and youngsters ride them to school or play on them in the park. Some adults even ride them to work!

68 STROLLER

Strollers were designed to transport older babies and small children. Strollers need to be light so that they are easy to push and fold up, but should also have strong brakes and tires for safety and a smooth ride.

69 ▷ FIRE ENGINE

Fire engines carry a variety of fire-fighting and rescue equipment, plus a huge tank of water. However, special onboard pumps enable them to use sea or lake water to use on a fire and the pumps can also help pump out floodwater.

70 ▷ AMBULANCE

Ambulances are able to travel at high speed to an injured person, using their sirens to warn other vehicles to get out of the way. On board, a specially trained crew uses medical equipment to care for the patient on the way to hospital.

71 ▷ POLICE CAR

Police forces use cars to patrol the streets, to reach an emergency, or to chase speeding motorists. The cars often have extra-powerful engines and feature special markings, lights, and sirens so people can easily identify them.

72 GLIDER

A glider is an aircraft without an engine. It is towed up into the air by a powered aircraft, after which the tow rope is released and the glider stays airborne by flying along pockets of rising air currents.

73 SEAPLANE

Seaplanes are aircraft that can take off and land on water. Some types look like normal planes but feature special floats instead of wheels, while others have bodies where the bottom of the fuselage is shaped like the hull of a boat.

74 HELICOPTER

Helicopters use rotor blades to lift off vertically from the ground, hover, and fly. As they can land in places where traditional aircraft can't, they are used by emergency services such as air ambulances and in air-sea rescues.

75 PASSENGER JET

Every year millions of vacationers and business people fly around the world on passenger planes. These aircraft have made the world a much smaller place since it now only takes hours to arrive at places that used to take days or weeks to reach.

76 ROCKET

The Saturn V rocket was built for the Apollo missions, which in 1969 achieved their goal of landing the first humans on the moon. Taller than a 36-story building, Saturn V was the largest, most powerful rocket ever built.

77 LANDING CRAFT

The landing craft is the part of the spacecraft that touches down on the moon's surface. The Apollo spacecraft was divided into three parts: the service module, the command module and the lunar module, which was the landing craft.

79 SPACE SHUTTLE

The first reusable spacecraft, the Space Shuttle launched like a rocket, carrying people into space for research or taking satellites into orbit or bringing them back for repairs. At the end of the assignment, it landed back on earth and was refitted for another mission.

78 JETPACK

Astronauts use jetpacks to move around outside space stations, using small blasts of nitrogen gas to steer and to stop them from drifting off into space. On earth, the technology has not yet been developed for us to fly with a jetpack!

80 MOON BUGGY

The moon buggy's official name was the Lunar Roving Vehicle or LRV. This battery-powered buggy transported astronauts and their equipment across the surface of the moon. Three LRVs were left behind . . . and are still one the moon!

45

How would you travel?

KATY HALFORD

Katy Halford is an illustrator based in Leicestershire, UK. Her love of drawing started when she was small and continued right through school and university. She graduated from Loughborough University with a degree in Illustration and is now a full-time Illustrator.

Katy's work always starts in her sketchbook where she dreams up illustrated characters and imaginary worlds. Observing nature and people-watching are two of Katy's favorite sources of inspiration—she's always looking for ideas in her everyday world! Her colored artworks are mostly digital, but from time to time she creates and scans patterns and textures to use in her work.

DK | Penguin Random House

Illustrated by Katy Halford
Written by Henrietta Drane
Created and designed for DK by Plum5 Ltd

Senior Editor Elizabeth Yeates
Editor Phil Hunt
US Senior Editor Shannon Beatty
Managing Art Editor Gemma Glover
Senior Producer, Pre-Production Nikoleta Parasaki
Senior Producer Amy Knight
Jacket Coordinator Francesca Young
Creative Technical Support Sonia Charbonnier
Art Director Helen Senior
Publishing Director Sarah Larter

First American Edition, 2018
Published in the United States by DK Publishing
345 Hudson Street, New York, New York 10014

Copyright © 2018 Dorling Kindersley Limited
DK, a Division of Penguin Random House LLC
18 19 20 21 22 10 9 8 7 6 5 4 3 2 1
001–310324–Nov/2018

A catalog record for this book
is available from the Library of Congress
ISBN: 978-1-4654-7572-5

DK books are available at special discounts when purchased in bulk for sales promotions, premiums, fund-raising, or educational use. For details, contact: DK Publishing Special Markets, 345 Hudson Street, New York, New York 10014
SpecialSales@dk.com

Printed in China

A WORLD OF IDEAS:
SEE ALL THERE IS TO KNOW

www.dk.com